COMPENDIUM
CLASSIC LIVING

BETA-PLUS

COMPENDIUM
CLASSIC LIVING

January 2009

ISBN 13: 978-90-8944-011-2

2
A project by
Costermans.

4-5
This spacious villa with
adjoining pool house
was built by Vlassak-
Verhulst and
completely renovated
and restyled by
Alexander Cambron
(also see photograph
on p. 12–13 and report
on p. 16–59).

CONTENTS

FOREWORD

Classic living in all its aspects: from a restored, intimate farmhouse to a stately home, from a distinctive country estate to a timeless apartment.

The reader will undoubtedly find a lot of inspiration for the design and furnishing of his own classic interior on the basis of twenty projects from prominent interior design experts.

Wim Pauwels
Publisher

The bathroom (with bluestone bath surround)

in a seaside home created by Vlassak-Verhulst.

PART I

INSPIRATIONAL CREATIONS

THE RENOVATION
OF AN EXCLUSIVE DREAM HOME

Following a successful career in business, Alexander Cambron now creates around three completely ready-to-use, top-quality residential projects a year, in both contemporary and timelessly classic designs. These are "pret-à-habiter" homes for top executives and their families, with the focus entirely on the wishes and requirements of the new owners. The homes provide the ideal setting for the hobbies of the lady and gentleman of the house, a paradise for the children, ample space for sport and relaxation, a fully wired home office, a collection of cars and a workshop, a wine cellar, home-automation systems, music and security and a beautiful fully grown garden with space for a horse and pets.

The founder of the company coordinates these exclusive projects from start to finish, in collaboration with renowned architects, offering the elegant homes for sale only after all of the furnishing and decoration has been completed.

The exclusive country home in this report, originally designed by Vlassak-Verhulst, is a perfect illustration of this philosophy and mode of working. The interior was created by Fabienne Dupont.

This classic villa, with its typical chimney beside the main entrance, is English in inspiration. The driveway is in "rossekop" cobblestones.

20-21

A harmony of colour in the grey rendered finish of the walls, the weathered ipé wood and the grey-tinted garage doors.

24-27

A combination of reclaimed tiles for the house and a thatched roof for the swimming pool.

The English-style garden, full of flowers and pruned bushes.

22

The south-facing country garden with terraces in aged afrormosia wood and old Dutch clinker bricks, with a variety of flowers and plants.

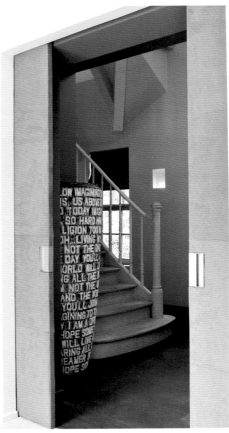

The modern look of the interior contrasts with the classic house. The impressive entrance hall occupies the full height of the building.

30-31

A seamless combination of classic and contemporary elements in the sitting room.

The home office has a calm atmosphere, with its view of the surrounding greenery. On the other side of the see-through fireplace are the home cinema and the second sitting room. The living and working areas are connected, but doors can be used to separate them if required.

34-35

A parquet floor in bleached oak (30cm boards) in this space between the sitting room and the office.

A multi-purpose space containing a secretary's desk, meeting room and a home office with a view of the entrance and the green surroundings.

In the kitchen, Fabienne Dupont has combined dark oak veneer with splashes of bright red.

The red cupboard doors also
lend extra colour and
dynamism to this kitchen.

42-43
A suede-covered sliding
wall separates the
kitchen and dining room.

44-47

The health and relaxation space, with a gym, hammam, jacuzzi and a swimming pool with a floor that can be raised to turn the space into a reception area.

The large sliding doors open onto the sun deck and fill this space with light.

This long, open corridor leads to the bedrooms and looks out over the entrance hall.

The master bedroom in black and white with an open fireplace connecting the dressing room and bedroom. All of the rooms have a view of the back garden.

The black dressing room of the master suite is in oak veneer, with a see-through gas fire.

The colour-coordinated bathroom in beige natural stone with illuminated white onyx walls beside the bath and in the shower.

56-57
An overflow bath with a ceiling-mounted tap. The sliding doors are in leather, in the same colour as the stone.

Three children's rooms and
bathrooms with playful details:
heart-shaped mirrors, an
illuminated bath and wall, and
pebble tiles. A few touches of
bright colour, with the rest painted
white.

The car museum,
the wine cellar and the
cloakroom of the house.

Alexander Cambron
mail@alexandercambron.be

Fabienne Dupont
Interior Decoration
fabienne.dupont@skynet.be

A COSY HOME IN SOLID WOOD

With seventy-five employees and around seventy projects a year in Belgium and northern France, wood construction company Mi Casa has become a familiar name in the markets for turnkey homes and wood construction.

Mi Casa is celebrating its fifteenth anniversary in 2008. The company has opted to invest in new technology for the entire construction process, in order to remain competitive and to improve quality. They also plan to introduce other modern techniques to upgrade their homes, such as new insulation and ventilation technology. This year Mi Casa is also bringing out its own line of furniture, which is designed in the same spirit as their wooden houses. They are converting one of their show homes, "Het Blauwe Huis" (The Blue House), for use as a display area, where visitors can take a good look at the kitchens, dressing rooms and furniture.

This report features one of Mi Casa's most recent projects: the perfect example of a classic, stylish home where the focus is on quality of life and a cosy, enjoyable living environment.

62-65

This recent Mi Casa creation is one of the many wooden homes that the company has constructed in New England, America.

Since 1995, these houses have formed an original and refreshing alternative, in contrast with many new farmhouse-style buildings. Mi Casa is still associated with this type of home nowadays, even though the company has also been building solid wood homes in other classic and modern architectural styles for a long time now.

66-69

A Mi Casa home has a maximum of two floors, plus an attic and a cellar. This type of solid wood structure is a stable house that can cope perfectly with the vertical load of its own weight, the roof and the interior, as well as the horizontal load of the wind.

Solid wood houses make stylish, cosy and timeless homes.

Mi Casa uses the time-honoured technique of the dovetail joint in the construction of its homes. They pile solid wooden beams on top of one another, connecting them with a tongue and groove method and securing them at each corner. This approach means that there are no crossing beams, so the interior walls are not interrupted, and the cavity insulation can extend through the exterior walls.

The interior walls are made of solid wood beams in Norway red pine and the exterior is in brick or cedar wood, depending on local construction regulations.

76-79

Some of the major advantages of wood construction are the architectural freedom, the dry construction and the speed of completion.

Another selling point for solid wood is its good insulation properties. Thanks to its porous nature and its low bulk density, wood insulates seven times better than brick or stone. In combination with well-insulated glass and insulation material in the roof, the floor and between the interior and exterior walls, wood construction can ensure that energy consumption is up to thirty per cent lower than in a traditional house. This construction method also provides good sound proofing, with a double layer of sound proofing between the floors and a five-centimetre-thick floating floor.

Additional insulation and the intrinsic thermal properties of wood mean that the house heats up quickly in cold weather, while staying cool when the weather is hot. The result: energy saving and a comfortable home.

The many advantages of construction with solid wood mean that this technique, in which Mi Casa has developed great expertise, is synonymous with healthy living.

Mi Casa does not only wish to construct houses that are safe, functional, durable and comfortable. The company also strives to create beautiful, personalised homes, in which the architecture and decoration reflect the philosophy and wishes of the owners. The wood of the Norway red pine exhibits more natural warmth and charm than the wood of local trees.

Their natural appearance means that wooden walls require little decoration. The owner immediately feels at home because the walls do not seem bare and unfinished or cause the room to echo unpleasantly.

For fifteen years Mi Casa has combined functionality and aesthetics with top-quality construction and completion.

Mi Casa

    Deerlijkseweg 218

    B – 8790 Waregem

    T +32 (0)56 60 79 95

    F +32 (0)56 60 99 97

    www.micasa.be

    micasa@micasa.be

    Show home:

    Natiënlaan 178

    B – 8300 Knokke-Heist

A MIXTURE OF STYLES

Any homeowner who wants his property renovated is right to have high expectations of the contractor.

The requirements can often be summarised in one sentence: complete the project within a reasonable period of time and a realistic budget, using top-quality materials that express the owners' individuality and make them feel at home. The modern building contractor often switches and mixes different styles, with one project influencing another.

Construmax has an instinctive understanding of customers' needs, aiming to lead each of its clients quickly and painlessly through the building process.

The projects in this report are a perfect illustration of the company's approach.

The materials used in this kitchen, in a suburban terraced house, create a cosy country atmosphere.

Construmax used oak fronts, combined with bluestone surfaces and a multi-coloured terracotta floor.

This bathroom has a walk-in shower with mosaic tiles, large glass screens and designer taps. The simple lines are retained throughout, even in the light fittings. The colours white and grey also help to create a calm, cool look.

Modern contractors are constantly inspired by the cross-fertilisation between the projects they create, and so different styles are often effortlessly mixed within a single apartment, at the owners' request.

This home is a perfect example of such a mixture of styles. The owners wanted modern and simple lines, without having to lose any of the rustic warmth of their home. The country charm of this house can be seen in the wooden floor and window frames. The modern touches come from the construction of a Gyproc partition wall with a built-in fireplace and by the owners' choice of furniture and decoration.

The bathroom also has the same modern look without too many frills. The straight lines here are interrupted only by the rounded shape of the washbasins, the warm lighting and the fun lettering on the shower wall.

CONSTRUMAX
info@construmax.be
www.construmax.be
T +32 (0)475 46 00 58
F +32 (0)3 218 86 49

THE RESTORATION OF THE HISTORIC CRETENBURGHOEVE

The Cretenburghoeve is a listed building dating back to the eighteenth century (1771).
The building had fallen into disrepair and urgent restoration was needed to prevent collapse.

Pas-partoe interiors took care of the work inside the farmhouse, while architect K. Beeck, a specialist in the restoration of historic buildings, coordinated the exterior work. Ballmore landscaped the garden.

Pas-partoe created a bright, open home, which has a simple appearance, yet uses classic, high-quality materials.
The company created clean views through the building by concealing any elements, such as radiators, that might disturb the lines.

The restoration work took two years. Some sections of the building had to be carefully dismantled and then painstakingly rebuilt, including walls, roof trusses, floors and the roof itself.

The result: a distinctive historic farmhouse has been beautifully restored to its former glory.

102-107

Chair supplied by pas-partoe.

The red one-seater is an LCW chair by Eames.

The table in the sitting room is a Piet Boon design.

108-111

Sandblasted oak is combined with smooth bluestone in the kitchen. A large sliding panel conceals the kitchen appliances. The custom-made table is based on a design by pas-partoe.

The organic form of the "Tulip" chairs by Eero Saarinen contrasts with the straight lines of the fitted kitchen units and table.

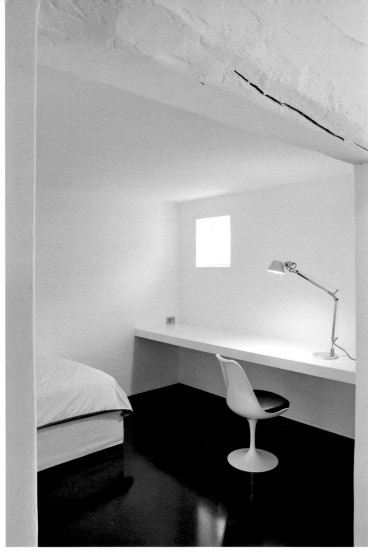

A view of the children's rooms with an Orizzonti bed.
The fitted wardrobes and desk are finished in a zinc-based
paint.

A stainless-steel football table by RS Barcelona
with hand-painted figures.

The parents' bedroom, also with an Orizzonti bed.

Standing lamp from pas-partoe.

Shower in marble mosaic with Vola taps.

Indirect light behind the mirrors.

Exposed roof beams in the attic. Sisal floor
covering. Stairs in polished concrete.

pas-partoe

Dorpsplein 2

B – 2830 Heindonk (Mechelen)

T +32 (0)3 866 40 66

www.pas-partoe.be

info@pas-partoe.be

A COUNTRY HOME
FOR EVERY STAGE OF LIFE

This completely customised country house is a total-concept project by architect Annik Dierckx and can be adapted to suit different stages of life, from a young working family to a retired couple with reduced mobility.

The architect designed every detail of the architecture and the interior, so that all of the elements are perfectly attuned, creating a home with an atmosphere of harmony and serenity.
Classic elements have been combined with modern design throughout this house.

This entrance hall is a surprisingly light and welcoming space, with its high ceilings and doors and interplay between natural and artificial light coming from a variety of sources including upstairs windows and lighting built into the stair rail.
A clearly laid-out circulation route connects the entrance hall directly with all of the major rooms on the ground floor.

A double oak door leads from the entrance hall into the living room. A perpendicular axis runs from the front door to the sitting room, all the way through to the open fireplace. Fire is an important element in the living areas.

The living room runs through into the dining room and the television room. The television room has a gas fireplace.

From the dining table, you can see the fire in the television room, because all of the rooms are connected.

The large sliding doors in the oak wall can separate the television room from the sitting and dining room if required.

124-127

The kitchen/dining room is in the wooden barn adjoining the main brick volume of the house. The fully glazed wall opens out onto the terrace and garden. The table-height open fire gives the room a warm, cosy atmosphere. The classic oak beams, combined with the glossy white of the kitchen, create a look that is both original and timeless.

The parents' bedroom is reached via the dressing room, which also provides access to the main bathroom and the library. A sliding panel creates a connection between the bedroom and bathroom. The witty antique chandelier contrasts with the plain, dark-tinted oak units in the dressing room and bedroom.

The main bathroom, like the rest of the house, is completely accessible for wheelchairs. Dark-tinted oak has been used here too, for the bath surround and washbasin units. Sand on the beach was the inspiration for the bathroom floor. The textured sand-coloured ceramic tiles have a natural anti-slip finish.

The furniture in the guest room is in wengé. The tropical wood lends warmth to this space and to the adjoining bathroom.

The sturdy glass floor in the upstairs hallway allows light to flow through into the entrance hall below.

The symmetry of the main brick building gives it a stately appearance. The wooden barn, which houses the garages, laundry and kitchen, offers a contrast to the stateliness of the building and provides a rustic charm.

Annik Dierckx
Architect
Paleisstraat 120
B - 2018 Antwerp
annik.dierckx@skynet.be
MOB +32 (0)476 29 61 20
T +32 (0)3 248 45 49

A PASSION FOR AUTHENTICITY AND TIMELESS INTERIORS

Doran for Country Cooking designs and creates its own individual range of interior architecture for construction and renovation projects.

A team of interior architects and colour consultants works together to develop complete customised interiors.

These home concepts are always designed with a touch of timelessness and with a harmonious combination of forms and colours. Every element of the living concept is a unique piece.

Doran for Country Cooking builds complete interiors in contemporary and rustic styles, using the kitchen and dining area as a starting point. Traditional craftsmanship is the theme running through all of their projects.

The company designs customised interiors for every aspect of daily life, including living rooms, bathrooms, bedrooms and dressing rooms.

They see the balance between functionality and aesthetics as the key to successful home design.

Doran for Country Cooking follows this philosophy, adding a new dimension to every room.

This grand country home is a striking example of the company's approach.

Daring colour combinations in cosy surroundings with an atmosphere of warmth and conviviality.

An old-fashioned tap with a solid stone washbasin. Wooden unit by Doran.

The rustic-style linen room, with units in painted wood and a bluestone surface. Stone tiles on the floor from the "fleur de lys" collection.

142-147

The country kitchen with a cast-iron Nobel stove and oak units with bluestone surfaces. The traditionally produced wall tiles are part of the Doran collection.

The bathroom is equipped with a walk-in shower, fitted pine units and an oak door from the Doran collection.
The hinged three-part mirror has a moulded oak frame.

A bleached oak floor from the Doran collection.

Pine wall unit with an oak surface and a built-in linen cupboard.

The dressing-room cupboards are in painted MDF with an oak surface.

Doran for Country Cooking

Gerard Willemotlaan 104

B – 9030 Mariakerke

T +32 (0)9 269 02 98

F +32 (0)9 269 03 01

www.countrycooking.be

info@countrycooking.be

Showroom by appointment.

PART II

TIMELESSLY CLASSIC

THE CHARM OF AN ATMOSPHERIC COUNTRY HOUSE

English Heritage Buildings started designing and constructing oak carports and garages twelve years ago in the Benelux countries.
The company's list of projects has expanded considerably since then: pool houses, guest quarters, home offices and extensions.

The house in this report was built in the 1980s in an idyllic position on a hill in Grez-Doiceau (Walloon Brabant).
The owners gave Heritage Buildings carte blanche and asked them to extend the original building by creating a large living room, a TV room and a master bedroom.

For aesthetic reasons, the company decided to incorporate a height difference between the new living room and the television room, which gives the house a more attractive appearance from the outside.

The entire oak-wood structure has been secured with mortise and tenon joints, following time-honoured tradition.

This porch was constructed to prevent direct sunlight and heat on the south-facing side of the building. The window frames are in iroko wood, which will turn the same colour as the larch boards once it starts to age.

The master bedroom is behind the dormer window.

156

The walls and ceiling of the television room are painted dark grey.

The oak beams have been left untreated so as to create an atmosphere of rustic charm.

A large screen is concealed in the last oak beam and can be lowered in front of the cupboard unit if required.

Large French windows offer a magnificent view of the surrounding hilly landscape.

The new living room is completely in white, which provides the

perfect backdrop for the beautiful antiques.

The entire oak-wood structure is secured with mortise and tenon joints.

Heritage Buildings
Ambiorixlei 8b
B – 2900 Schoten
T +32 (0)3 685 20 00
F +32 (0)3 685 23 73
www.heritagebuildings.be

The height difference between the living room and the TV room makes this space much cosier.

TIMELESS AND SOPHISTICATED TOTAL CONCEPTS FOR THE INTERIOR

Trendson interiors have three generations of experience in interior decoration and window treatments, with the emphasis on creating flawless custom-made pieces in their own workshop.

Experts in upholstery materials and interior design, the Van Gestel-Clés, a husband-and-wife team, have in recent years concentrated increasingly on total concepts for the interior.

They devote great care and attention to selecting sophisticated window treatments, unusual wallpaper, exclusive furniture and atmospheric lighting, which they combine to create a unique atmosphere.

The Trendson directors Koen Van Gestel and Suzy Clé display their striking and timeless designs for complete decoration projects at "In den Posthoorn", a historic building, where art (dramatic paintings by Claire Basler and alabaster sculptures by Pascal Cerchi) and streamlined interior design combine in a unique way.

Trendson interieur creates a harmony of timeless home design with dramatic art by Claire Basler and alabaster sculpture by Pascal Cerchi.

The company combines internationally renowned furniture collections, such as Baker, Moissonnier and JNL in a variety of styles.

A cosy atmosphere with a textile wall
covering and exclusive fabrics.

Trendson interiors

" In den Posthoorn "

Schoutetstraat 4

B - 2800 Mechelen

T +32 (0) 15 210 260

www.trendson.be

info@trendson.be

Trendson art gallery

Joseph Stevensstraat 34

B - 1000 Brussels

www.trendson.be

A COMPLETE FACELIFT
FOR A SPACIOUS VILLA

Interior specialist Benedikte Lecot was commissioned to refurbish this large, exclusive villa.
This magnificent home offered many opportunities for renovation: Lecot completely rearranged the rooms and introduced an atmosphere of luxurious, contemporary comfort throughout the house.

This project is the perfect advertisement for Benedikte Lecot's expertise: an interior in which functionality, atmosphere, light and architecture are in absolute harmony. This is the ideal combination of classic and modern in a distinctive, cosy and timeless setting.

The old, gilded balustrade and the chandelier have been sprayed

black and a fitted carpet was removed from the stairs.

Painted skirting boards replaced the French Massangis stone wall

tiles. A pedestal was provided for the statue in the background.

The extra-long sofa is in proportion with the length of the sitting room.

Lecot converted two rooms with small windows into one large room with big windows. The oak grille in the bluestone floor is for heating and cooling the room.

A bluestone sink with a copper tap.

The upstairs rooms were completely redesigned.

A dressing room and a large bathroom were needed. Lecot created a suite for the parents of the family,

including a spacious bedroom and bathroom.

Lecot selected pale colours for the children's rooms: grey for the son and pink for the daughter, with both colours in harmony with the wooden floor.

Benedikte Lecot

Kuurnsestraat 44 B

B – 8860 Lendelede

T +32 (0)495 29 28 39

F +32 (0)51 32 07 28

www.b-lecot.be

interiors@b-lecot.be

EXCLUSIVE "À LA CARTE" INTERIORS

Ter Poel Interieur carries out and coordinates complete renovation projects.

All of the work is done on an "à la carte" basis, with the perfect finish reinforcing the exclusive character of every interior.

Ter Poel Interieur combines atmosphere, light, form and colour, with a perfect eye for the correct mix of the various elements.

Ter Poel has carried out a number of total projects in Grindelwald, Switzerland.

Ter Poel Interieur
T +32 (0)475 81 46 74
www.terpoelinterieur.com
info@terpoelinterieur.com

A TASTE FOR HARMONIOUS, HIGH-QUALITY LIVING

In the past, furniture was often made to order by passionate and dedicated cabinetmakers, but this way of working is no longer common.

This passion, passed on from generation to generation, can result in high-quality traditional craftsmanship of the kind that can be seen in the work of Frank Tack.

Frank Tack does not design and create only kitchens, but also complete customised interiors.

His enthusiasm for top-quality materials is reflected in every room he works on, creating a pleasant living environment where traditional methods and expertise are beautifully integrated into the home.

The owners' individual style and preferences are carefully discussed on a room-by-room basis, so that the perfect materials can be selected for each space.

The exclusive, durable wood that Tack uses also helps to create an atmosphere of elegance and comfort in his wonderfully harmonious designs.

Tack incorporated this staircase and hallway into the open living room, carefully attuning all of the different elements.

The radiator covers are pieces of furniture in their own right, designed to complement the panelling in this room.

The cupboard units make this a very versatile space.

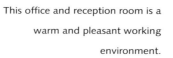

This office and reception room is a warm and pleasant working environment.

Every spot in the living room provides a different perspective of this restful home.

Frank Tack has developed a strong reputation as a designer and creator of timeless country kitchens.

The central, multifunctional island creates an interesting link between the kitchen and the dining area.

Once again, all of the materials are in perfect harmony.

Frank Tack reflects the owners' wishes and lifestyle in his complete interior designs.

Expert advice from design to creation results in interiors that are full of class and character.

Frank Tack

Kitchens and furniture

Design and production

Grotstraat 74

B – 8780 Oostrozebeke

T +32 (0)51 40 47 18

F +32 (0)51 40 61 40

76, avenue de Villiers

F – 75017 Paris

www.tack-keukens.be

www.franktack.eu

info@tack-keukens.be

CUSTOM-MADE TOTAL CONCEPTS IN EXCLUSIVE HOME CONSTRUCTION AND RENOVATION

The Aarschot-based family firm b+ villas has been in business for thirty-five years. As a leading developer of complete new-build, renovation and interior projects, b+ villas works in a wide variety of styles, from hypermodern to country classic, and always within the luxury sector.

The company's fully customised concepts comprise an extensive range of services, from design, construction and project management to the finishing touches, including interior design, decoration, garden landscaping and even maintenance. In all of its projects, the company always puts the wishes of its clients first.

This complete service guarantees that the company can satisfy all of the client's requirements and means that the customer only has to deal with one contractor.
The company's motto holds true: tell us how you want to live.
The development of a strong, personalised, long-term relationship with its clients forms an important part of the company's philosophy.
The top priority for b+ villas is client care, coupled with guaranteed quality and budget.

If you opt for b+ villas, you are choosing more than just a beautiful villa: these are dream homes that reflect the specific wishes of the owner, right down to the smallest details.

The construction of a classic *manoir*-style villa. The facade is in *crépi* rendering and reclaimed *paepesteen* bricks.

The kitchen and family room look out onto a covered terrace with overhead heating and a fireplace, which can be used until late in the autumn. The rear of the house has a stone terrace running along its entire length.

A smoothed bluestone floor made up of large tiles.

The dining room and living room flow smoothly together and are separated by a wall with storage space along both sides. A warm old-Flemish oak floor was selected for this space.

If required, b+ villas can also create and coordinate the entire interior design, as in this customised kitchen with adjoining family room.

A timeless, contemporary classic style that will only become more beautiful with time.

As an exclusive provider of luxury homes, b+ villas always works with long-lasting, high-quality materials, such as solid wood, natural stone and traditionally produced fabrics.

Custom-built bathroom in Emperador brown natural stone.

The hallway with a broad staircase in cerused oak and a wrought-iron door leading to the living room.

This classic villa is completely surrounded by a terrace and garden.

b+ villas carry out projects in Belgium and the southern Netherlands.

b+ villas

Nieuwlandlaan 19

B – 3200 Aarschot

T +32 (0)16 55 35 60

F +32 (0)16 55 35 61

www.bplusvillas.be

LUXURY AND SIMPLICITY
IN A TIMELESS APARTMENT

Costermans created this timeless luxury apartment, a stone's throw away from the town hall in a residential district near Antwerp, in cooperation with Jan des Bouvrie's Studio Het Arsenaal.

They created a powerful concept behind a classic Parisian-style facade, with key features including high ceilings, lots of light, and rooms that are spacious, yet cosy.

Natural shades and materials were used, combined with flashes of purple and lilac.

Art from the Arsenaal collection provides the finishing touch.

The large mirror with its flower design increases the sense of space in the entrance hall.

The classically inspired bench, upholstered in purple velvet, provides a cheerful note.

The living room has a cosy sitting area in front of the simple gas fire.
A streamlined design for the bookshelves behind the armchairs.

The cheerful cushions in
muted shades lend a
warm, playful touch to
the sitting room.
The shell lamps are by
Verner Panton.

The kitchen/dining room has a table made from reclaimed pallet wood. Handle-free doors in a glossy white finish, with a Corian surface.

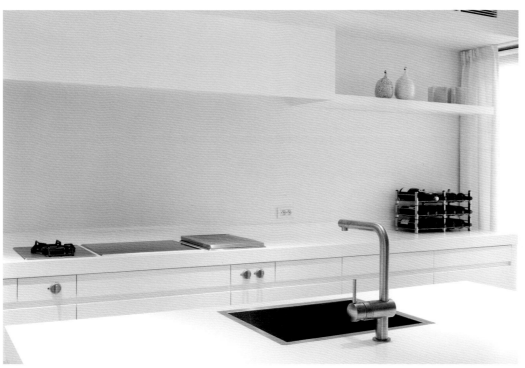

A harmony of Carrara marble and oak floorboards. The oak floor runs throughout the apartment, creating a sense of space and continuity.

A romantic bedroom
with a compact desk.

Costermans

Dwarsdreef 52

B – 2970 Schilde

T +32 (0)3 385 02 44

F +32 (0)3 384 29 66

www.costermans-projecten.be

info@costermans-projecten.be

Jan des Bouvrie

Studio Het Arsenaal B.V.

Kooltjesbuurt 1

NL – 1411 RZ Naarden

T +31 (0)35 694 11 44

F +31 (0)35 631 01 00

www.hetarsenaal.nl

PERFECTION EVEN IN THE DETAILS

The architectural fittings department at Lerou Ijzerwaren, a family ironmongery company based in Bruges, specialises in fittings for doors and furniture, locks and security, pieces for restoration projects, and exclusive accessories for kitchens, bathrooms and cloakrooms. Their emphasis is on traditionally manufactured fittings for restorations and for modern projects.

The Lerou showroom is a treasure trove of information and inspiration for architects, interior designers, restorers and cabinetmakers who appreciate real craftsmanship. Private individuals are also very welcome.

This report focuses on a number of recent interiors and architectural projects with Lerou fittings.

Lerou has collections in a variety of metal alloys. Here, furniture knobs
in fine pewter, doorknobs in solid brass and handles in cast iron.

Lerou offers a very wide collection of classic taps with ceramic discs and classic-style showers with thermostats.

Handles for sliding doors are available in round and elongated shapes and in twenty different colours.

Solid cast fittings on and around the front door.

Solid cast bells, available in ten different sizes, are a Lerou speciality.

Wooden furniture knobs and handles, which can be painted.

A banker's lamp from Lerou's brass Nantucket Lighting collection.

Lerou stocks typical Belgian "railway" door handles from a variety of periods, in different sizes and designs. These pages feature a straight design (p. 224) and a conical design (p. 225, right).

A combination of aluminium and nickel, both matte and polished, as door/window fittings and for lighting.

Handles for sliding doors are available in round and elongated shapes and in twenty different colours.

A patinated brass tap with ceramic interior and hand-made washbasin.

A combination of modern furniture fittings and classic fittings for antique furniture.

A reproduction of a door-handle design from the first half of the twentieth century.

Lerou Ijzerwaren

Monnikenwerve 131

B – 8000 Brugge

T +32 (0)50 31 74 42

F +32 (0)50 31 01 60

www.lerou.com

info@lerou.com

An example of the solid cast fittings supplied by Lerou, including doorknobs, handles, house numbers, doorbells and lighting.

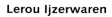

NEW LIFE FOR A BRIGHT
AND AIRY HOLIDAY HOME

Claudine Vasseur was asked to give a new lease of life to this holiday home on the Belgian coast.

The renovation work took ten months. Only the exterior walls and a couple of interior walls were left standing. The house was given a completely new roof, new plasterwork and a new terrace.

The owners wanted to have a very bright and airy home, with white as the basic colour. Their holiday home is a place for perfect relaxation.

Claudine Vasseur
Total Project Coordination
MOB +32 (0)475 72 08 71

This room functions as a children's cloakroom. It was created to provide direct access to the garden, so the children can run in and out as they please.
It is also the starting point for the parents' many long walks and cycle rides, so user-friendly Cotto d'Este tiles have been chosen for the floor.

230-233
The sitting room has two sections: a cosy area for welcoming guests, and a space for reading or watching television in front of the open fire. MDF bookshelves with indirect fluorescent lighting. The open fireplace is in metal, with a built-in guillotine screen.
The oak floor was hand-finished and treated with natural oil.
Matching coffee tables with a wrought-iron base and a surface in old oak.

EXCLUSIVE NATURAL STONE IN
A CLASSICALLY INSPIRED INTERIOR

Architect Christophe Decarpentrie designed this classically inspired interior with a dramatic style throughout the hall and in the bathrooms.

The Stonecompany, directed by Philippe Van den Weghe, supplied the stonework.

White Statuario marble was combined with golden-brown natural stone, both with a polished finish, in the hall and in the guest toilet.

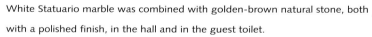

238-241

The main bathroom is in a combination of
Statuario (white marble) and Greek grey. Both
varieties of natural stone have a polished finish.

Crema Marfil and Greek Red Ritzona were chosen for the guest bathroom, again with a polished finish.

Van den Weghe

The Stonecompany

Statiestraat 69

B – 9870 Zulte

T +32 (0)9 388 83 00

F +32 (0)9 388 51 66

www.stonecompany.be

info@vandenweghe.be

ADDRESSES

A project by Mi Casa.

b+ villas
Nieuwlandlaan 19
B – 3200 Aarschot
T +32 (0)16 55 35 60
F +32 (0)16 55 35 61
www.bplusvillas.be
p. 192-207

Alexander Cambron
mail@alexandercambron.be
p. 16-59

Construmax
info@construmax.be
www.construmax.be
T +32 (0) 475 46 00 58
F +32 (0) 3 218 86 49
p. 92-99

Costermans
Dwarsdreef 52
B – 2970 Schilde
T +32 (0)3 385 02 44
F +32 (0)3 384 29 66
www.costermans-projecten.be
info@costermans-projecten.be
p. 208-219

Jan des Bouvrie
Studio Het Arsenaal B.V.
Kooltjesbuurt 1
NL – 1411 RZ Naarden
T +31 (0)35 694 11 44
F +31 (0)35 631 01 00
www.hetarsenaal.nl
p. 208-219

Annik Dierckx
Architect
Paleisstraat 120
B - 2018 Antwerp
annik.dierckx@skynet.be
MOB +32 (0)476 29 61 20
T +32 (0)3 248 45 49
p. 118-135

Doran for Country Cooking
Gerard Willemotlaan 104
B – 9030 Mariakerke
T +32 (0)9 269 02 98
F +32 (0)9 269 03 01
www.countrycooking.be
info@countrycooking.be
Showroom on appointment.
p. 136-151

Fabienne Dupont
Interior Decoration
Fabienne.dupont@skynet.be
p. 16-59

Heritage Buildings
Ambiorixlei 8b
B – 2900 Schoten
T +32 (0)3 685 20 00
F +32 (0)3 685 23 73
www.heritagebuildings.be
p. 154-161

Benedikte Lecot
Kuurnsestraat 44 B
B – 8860 Lendelede
T +32 (0)495 29 28 39
F +32 (0)51 32 07 28
www.b-lecot.be
interiors@b-lecot.be
p. 168-175

Lerou

Monnikenwerve 131

B – 8000 Brugge

T +32 (0)50 31 74 42

F +32 (0)50 31 01 60

www.lerou.com

info@lerou.com

p. 220-227

Mi Casa

Deerlijkseweg 218

B – 8790 Waregem

T +32 (0)56 60 79 95

F +32 (0)56 60 99 97

www.micasa.be

micasa@micasa.be

Showhouse:

Natiënlaan 178

B – 8300 Knokke-Heist

p. 60-91

pas-partoe

Dorpsplein 2

B – 2830 Heindonk (Mechelen)

T +32 (0)3 866 40 66

www.pas-partoe.be

info@pas-partoe.be

p. 100-117

Frank Tack

Kitchens and furniture

Concept and production

Grotstraat 74

B – 8780 Oostrozebeke

T +32 (0)51 40 47 18

F +32 (0)51 40 61 40

76, avenue de Villiers

F – 75017 Paris

www.tack-keukens.be

www.franktack.eu

info@tack-keukens.be

p. 184-191

Ter Poel Interiors

T +32 (0)475 81 46 74

www.terpoelinterieur.com

info@terpoelinterieur.com

p. 176-183

Trendson interiors

" In den Posthoorn "

Schoutetstraat 4

B - 2800 Mechelen

T +32 (0) 15 210 260

www.trendson.be

info@trendson.be

Trendson Art Gallery

Joseph Stevensstraat 34

B - 1000 Brussels

www.trendson.be

p. 162-167

Claudine Vasseur

Total Project Coordination

MOB +32 (0)475 72 08 71

p. 228-233

Van den Weghe

The Stonecompany

Statiestraat 69

B – 9870 Zulte

T +32 (0)9 388 83 00

F +32 (0)9 388 51 66

www.stonecompany.be

info@vandenweghe.be

p. 234-243

252-253

A project by

Alexander Cambron

and Fabienne Dupont.

PUBLISHER

BETA-PLUS Publishing

Termuninck 3

B - 7850 Enghien (Belgium)

T. +32 (0)2 395 90 20

F. +32 (0)2 395 90 21

www.betaplus.com

info@betaplus.com

PHOTOGRAPHY

All pictures: Jo Pauwels, except:

p. 162-167 Jean-Pierre Gabriel

p. 168-175 Claude Smekens

p. 192-207 © b+ villas

GRAPHIC DESIGN

POLYDEM bvba

Nathalie Binart

TRANSLATION

Laura Watkinson

January 2009

ISBN 13: 978-90-8944-011-2